SPECIAL NEEDS SUPPORT AND FUNDING GUIDE

SPECIAL NEEDS SUPPORT AND FUNDING GUIDE

167 Lesser-known Grants, Resources and Services for Families & Caregivers to Reduce Costs, Alleviate Stress, and Help Their Children Thrive

Andrea Campbell

Pocket Learner Publishing

© Copyright Andrea Campbell 2024 - All rights reserved.

The content contained in this book may not be reproduced, duplicated, or transmitted without direct written permission from the author or publisher.

Under no circumstances will any blame or legal responsibility be held against the publisher or author for any damages, reparation, or monetary loss due to the information contained within this book, either directly or indirectly. You are responsible for your own choices, actions, and results.

Legal Notice:

This book is copyright-protected and is only for personal use. You cannot amend, distribute, sell, use, quote, or paraphrase any part of this book's content without the author's or publisher's consent.

Disclaimer Notice:

Please note that the information contained in this text is for educational and entertainment purposes only. All effort has been executed to present accurate, up-to-date, and reliable, complete information. No warranties of any kind are declared or implied. Readers acknowledge that the author is not engaging in rendering legal, financial, medical, or professional advice. The content within this book has been derived from various sources. Please consult a licensed professional before attempting any techniques outlined in this book.

ISBN: 978-1-914997-43-3 (sc)

Table of Contents

Introduction vii

Part I - The United States of America 1

Part 2 - Canada 27

Part 3 - The United Kingdom 51

International Grants 77

Conclusion 79

Resources 82

Introduction

When caring for a child with special needs, families often encounter challenges, including financial burdens and emotional stress. Yet, amidst these trials, a wealth of untapped support is waiting to be discovered and accessed. This book is more than just a guide; it's a beacon of hope, crafted with care and offering invaluable insights and signposts that empower families and caregivers to provide optimum care for their children.

You will find in this brief text several lesser-known resources, provisions, and amenities available to families of children with special needs and disabilities. The book focuses on families in the United States, the

Introduction

United Kingdom, and Canada; however, families living in other regions should know that some of the organizations mentioned operate in multiple countries. I encourage these families to explore opportunities in their locations to find similar services for their children.

While some parents in the target regions are familiar with mainstream support services and benefits, there exist myriad hidden gems that can significantly enhance the lives of children with additional needs and their caregivers. Identifying and accessing the range of services and support systems for children with special needs can often be overwhelming and daunting. Families may grapple with complex bureaucracies, searching tirelessly for assistance that suits their children's unique requirements. This book provides valuable information for enriching children with disabilities and their families.

By revealing these sources of support, I hope to empower families with the knowledge needed to access the assistance, services, and amenities that can enhance their children's lives and foster a sense of inclusion,

Introduction

belonging, and well-being. I recognize that there are often challenges in deciphering the range of resources and services and that the application processes can be onerous. Still, I hope you will have the resilience to persevere in your quest for support. This book provides information about existing resources, but as parents and caregivers, you must take appropriate and consistent action to obtain the support you and your child deserve. From specialized therapies to educational input, each entry in this guide is carefully selected to provide relief where it's needed most.

My personal story served as the inspiration for this book. My daughter, who has a dual diagnosis of Down Syndrome and Autism Spectrum Disorder, requires additional care and attention, including frequent visits to care professionals, a tailored curriculum, and assistance with self-care. We realized early that our lives would change as we embraced the roles of caregivers and advocates. My family had to adjust our routines and revisit our goals as we leaned into our new reality. The experience led to a steep learning curve, and we missed out on many benefits in the early years simply because we were unaware of their existence.

Introduction

When we started to network with other parents, we realized that a range of support was accessible. The information in the book is not exhaustive, but I hope it will encourage you to be proactive in finding those benefits and sources of support that could help your family promote your child's development.

My life as a primary caregiver for our daughter attests to the fact that perseverance pays. After extensive research, hours of conversation with families and professionals, and pages of applications, we accessed a fair amount of support for our little girl. For example, when her school refused to conduct an educational assessment, we sourced it, contributing a minimal amount to the cost.

Over the years, we have received funding for household appliances, exercise equipment, respite care, travel costs, holidays, days out, and other amenities. It was not always easy to obtain, and we did not get everything we wanted, but we got enough. In addition, we helped other families access these benefits. We are relentless in our efforts to find support for our daughter as she approaches adulthood. Ours is an ongoing, perhaps never-ending journey, but the little, consistent wins make it all worthwhile.

I have put what I learned from this experience into this book and the other books I wrote for families of children with special needs and disabilities. In addition to government programs, you will find obscure funding opportunities and financial packages to access specialized therapies, recreational opportunities, and community amenities.

These resources, which have eluded countless families, can alleviate the economic burden, covering medical expenses, assistive devices, and specialist education. You will also find sources of support for advocacy, counseling, and respite care—resources that will benefit your emotional and physical health.

While the organizations and resources presented here are thoughtfully selected to help you, I also encourage you to seek personalized advice from professionals competent to offer tailored guidance. I have compiled

Introduction

this list of sources that currently provide support, but as time progresses, the status of some entities may change. However, remember that other help will always be available–parent groups, online forums, blog articles, journals, and web pages dedicated to your child's diagnosis.

I invite you to explore these options and opportunities in your locale and wider field. Use this guide as a launchpad for more profound, consistent research to find support that benefits your child and family. You can also obtain information from community organizations and resource centers such as libraries, places of worship, schools, medical centers, and extra-curricular activity venues.

In my experience as the parent of a child with special needs, the most impactful information has come from caregivers. I have found strength in connecting with other parents, learning from their experiences, and sharing my knowledge. All these activities help us understand the unique aspects of our role as caregivers of someone with special needs. I encourage you to

Introduction

connect with parents at the school gate, in social settings, and specialist forums, whether online or in person. It is helpful, reassuring, and comforting to share your experiences with people who understand your path.

Remember, you're not alone on this journey; a community of individuals and organizations exists to support families like yours. As we take steps along the extraordinary path of caring for our special children, let's access the help available, embrace the challenges, celebrate the victories, and support one another to create a world that embraces and empowers children and adults with special needs.

Part I - The United States of America

"It is easier to build strong children than to repair broken men."

— *Frederick Douglass, American abolitionist and orator*

The intricacies of the American healthcare, educational, and social systems can be complex, especially when seeking assistance for individuals with unique requirements.

Many organizations in the USA are responsible for providing special needs services, which are readily identifiable online. You may already be familiar with the benefits to which you may be entitled under the following Government programs and initiatives.

The USA

- ❖ Office of Special Education Programs (OSEP), whose remit it is to ensure access to fair, equitable, and high-quality education and services for children with disabilities. (https://www2.ed.gov/about/offices/list/osers/index.html)

- ❖ Special Needs Alliance, which runs government programs that offer grants or financial assistance for families with special needs. (https://www.specialneedsalliance.org/blog/government-programs-for-children-with-disabilities)

- ❖ US Government Social Security Disability Benefits (https://www.usa.gov/social-security-disability) offers benefits through Social Security Disability Insurance (SSDI) or Supplemental Security Income (SSI) if you have a disability.

If you are unfamiliar with the above, please take the time to investigate how your child could benefit from these mainstream sources of support. There are many reliable articles and guidance online about how to apply. Bear in mind that different states may have different procedures for applying.

In the following section, I provide insights into those lesser-known, inconspicuous sources of support that you can access if your child resides in the USA.

1 - Able Flight

Offers scholarships and training for individuals with disabilities to become licensed pilots through flight and aviation career training.

Website: https://ableflight.org

2 - ACT Today!

Provides grants for autism treatment, therapy, and support services.

Website: https://www.act-today.org

---

3 - Adopt America Network

Offers financial assistance and resources for families adopting children with disabilities.

Website: https://www.adoptamericanetwork.org

---

4 - Aplastic Anemia and MDS International Foundation

Provides resources, support, and advocacy for individuals with aplastic anemia and myelodysplastic syndromes (MDS).

Website: https://www.aamds.org

---

5 - Angelman Syndrome Foundation

Provides resources, support, and advocacy for individuals with Angelman Syndrome and their families.

Website: https://www.angelman.org

6 - Association of Blind Citizens

Offers financial aid and resources for individuals who are blind or visually impaired. The ABC offers assistance by providing information and referral, advocacy, and other supports to maximize and increase options and opportunities for all blind and or legally blind persons.

Website: https://blindcitizens.org

---

7 - Autism Speaks

Offers resources, advocacy, and support for individuals with autism spectrum disorders and their families.

Website: https://www.autismspeaks.org

---

8 - Canines for Disabled Kids

Provides service dogs to children with disabilities to increase independence and improve quality of life.

Website: https://caninesforkids.org

---

9 - Cure Duchenne

Supports research and provides family support for individuals with Duchenne muscular dystrophy.

Website: https://www.cureduchenne.org

---

10 - Cerebral Palsy Foundation

Provides resources, support, and advocacy for individuals with cerebral palsy and their families.

Website: https://www.yourcpf.org

---

11 - Challenged Athletes Foundation

Assists individuals with physical disabilities in participating in sports and recreational activities. The individual's permanent disability must impair mobility, affect the neuromuscular system, impair balance, or motor control.

Website: https://www.challengedathletes.org

---

12 - CHARGE Syndrome Foundation

Offers resources, support, and advocacy for individuals with CHARGE syndrome and their families.

Website: https://www.chargesyndrome.org

---

13 - Childhood Apraxia of Speech Association (CASANA)

Offers resources, support, and advocacy for children with apraxia of speech and their families.

Website: https://www.apraxiakids.org

---

14 - Cure SMA

Supports research, provides family support, and funds care initiatives for spinal muscular atrophy (SMA).

Website: https://www.curesma.org

---

15 - Cystic Fibrosis Foundation

Provides resources, support, and advocacy for individuals with cystic fibrosis and their families.

Website: https://www.cff.org

---

16 - Dravet Syndrome Foundation

Offers resources, research funding, and support for individuals with Dravet Syndrome and their families.

Website: https://www.dravetfoundation.org

---

17 - Dup15q Alliance

Offers resources, support, and advocacy for individuals with chromosome 15q duplications and their families.

Website: https://www.dup15q.org

---

18 - Family Voices

Provides resources and support for families with children who have special healthcare needs.

Website: https://www.familyvoices.org

---

19 - Friends of Disabled Adults and Children (FODAC)

Provides durable medical equipment, assistive technology, and home modifications for individuals with disabilities.

Website: https://www.fodac.org

---

20 - Fragile X Association of America

Offers resources, support, and advocacy for individuals with Fragile X Syndrome and their families.

Website: https://fragilex.org

21 - Global Down Syndrome Foundation

Provides medical care, research, advocacy and support for individuals with Down Syndrome.

Website: https://www.globaldownsyndrome.org

---

22 - International Dyslexia Association

Support: Offers resources, support, and advocacy for individuals with dyslexia and their families.

Website: https://dyslexiaida.org

---

23 - Little Lobbyists

Advocates for children with complex medical needs and disabilities, ensuring access to healthcare and support services.

Website: https://littlelobbyists.org

---

24 - Little People of America (LPA)

Provides support, resources, and scholarships for individuals with dwarfism and their families.

Website: https://www.lpaonline.org

25 - Loeys-Dietz Syndrome Foundation

Provides resources, support, and advocacy for individuals with Loeys-Dietz Syndrome and their families.

Website: https://www.loeysdietz.org

---

26 - Maggie Welby Foundation

The Maggie Welby Foundation provides grants to families with a specific goal in mind. That goal could be financial assistance with medical bills, modifying your vehicle to be wheelchair accessible, or even just pursuing an opportunity that wouldn't be available to your child otherwise.

Website: https://www.maggiewelby.org

---

27 - Modest Needs

Provides short-term financial assistance to individuals and families in temporary crisis who, because they are working and live just above the poverty level, are ineligible for most types of conventional social assistance.

Website: https://www.modestneeds.org

28 - Mobility Works

Provides a list of grants and funding sources from every state for people with disabilities who need assistance with purchasing or modifying a vehicle or other disability assistance.

Website: https://www.mobilityworks.com

---

29 - Muscular Dystrophy Association (MDA)

Offers resources, research funding, and support for individuals with muscular dystrophy and related diseases.

Website: https://www.mda.org

---

30 - National Ataxia Foundation

Offers resources, research funding, and support for individuals with ataxia.

Website: https://ataxia.org

---

31 - National Fragile X Foundation

Provides resources, support, and advocacy for individuals with Fragile X Syndrome.

Website: https://fragilex.org

32 - National Disability Institute

Offers resources and assistance to help those with disabilities and chronic health conditions build their financial resilience and navigate through difficult times.

Website: https://www.nationaldisabilityinstitute.org

---

33 - National Organization for Rare Disorders (NORD)

Provide patient assistance programs to help individuals living with rare diseases obtain medication, receive financial help with insurance premiums, get diagnostic testing assistance, receive travel assistance for clinical trials or consultation with disease specialists and provide caregiver respite.

Website: https://rarediseases.org

---

34 - Dysphonia International

Provides resources, support and advocacy for individuals with spasmodic dysphonia and related voice disorders.

Website: https://dysphonia.org

35 - Need Help Paying Bills

A website that provides information on various programs and resources that can help people with disabilities pay their bills, such as Social Security Disability Insurance (SSDI), Supplemental Security Income (SSI), Medicare, Medicaid waivers, energy assistance, housing assistance and more.

Website: https://www.needhelppayingbills.com

---

36 - Oracle Health Foundation

Provides funding for children whose families can't afford medical care, equipment, vehicle modifications or displacement related to care.

Website: https://www.oraclehealthfoundation.org

---

37 - Pacer Center

Provides resources, support, and advocacy for children with disabilities and their families. Provides individual assistance, workshops, publications, and other resources to help families decide about education and other services for their child or young adult with disabilities.

Website: https://www.pacer.org

38 - Prader-Willi Syndrome Association (USA)

Provides resources, support, and advocacy for individuals with Prader-Willi Syndrome, their families and caregivers.

Website: https://www.pwsausa.org

---

39 - Parent Project Muscular Dystrophy

Provides resources and research funding to ensure every family has access to expert healthcare providers, cutting edge treatments, and a community of support.

Website: https://www.parentprojectmd.org

---

40 - Project Mend

Provides professionally refurbished and sanitized medical equipment and other assistive technology items to individuals of all ages who are living with a disability and/or illness in South Texas.

Website: https://www.projectmend.org

---

41 - The Ray Tye Medical Aid Foundation

Funds in-hospital treatment and surgeries for those without health insurance or adequate financial means.

Website: https://www.rtmaf.org

---

42 - Smile Train

Offers financial assistance for cleft palate surgeries and related healthcare services.

Website: https://www.smiletrain.org

---

43 - Special Kids Fund

Provides vehicles to families of special needs children across the nation. Their Wheelchair Van Assistance Program help needy families' nationwide access handicap vans for their disabled family member.

Website: https://specialkidsfund.org

---

44 - Spina Bifida Association

Offers resources, support, research and advocacy for individuals with spina bifida and their families.

Website: https://www.spinabifidaassociation.org

---

45 - Starlight Children's Foundation

Provides entertainment through gaming, therapeutic play, toys and equipment for children in hospitals with serious illnesses and disabilities.

Website: https://www.starlight.org

---

46 - Sturge-Weber Foundation

Offers support through 25 centers that provide the comprehensive care necessary for treating adults and children who have a port wine (PW) birthmark, Sturge-Weber syndrome (SWS), or Klippel- Trenaunay (KT).

Website: https://sturge-weber.org

---

47 - TACA (The Autism Community in Action)

Offers comprehensive information and resources, monthly virtual parent support, educational events and parent mentorship for parents living with autism.

Website: https://tacanow.org

---

48 - The Arc

Offers resources, advocacy, and support services for individuals with intellectual and developmental disabilities. It has hundreds of local chapters that provide various services and programs, such as education, employment, housing, health and more.

Website: https://thearc.org

---

49 - The Different Needz Foundation

Helps individuals with developmental disabilities obtain the necessary equipment and medical services they need to have the best quality of life. The Foundation considers future needs and provides payment for medical services or equipment directly to the provider.

Website: http://www.differentneedzfoundation.org

---

50 - The Parker Lee Project

Works to cover the costs of equipment and medical treatment that your insurance may not. It also serves as a great educational resource and support system for parents with disabled children.

Website: http://www.theparkerleeproject.org

---

51 - Tourette Association of America

Provides resources, support, and advocacy for individuals with Tourette Syndrome and tic disorders.

Website: https://tourette.org

---

52 - Trisomy 18 Foundation

Provides support, resources, and advocacy for individuals with Trisomy 18 (Edwards syndrome) and their families.

Website: https://www.trisomy18.org

---

53 - United Cerebral Palsy (UCP)

Offers financial assistance and advocacy for children with cerebral palsy and other developmental disabilities.

Website: https://ucp.org

---

54 - United Healthcare Children's Foundation

Offers medical grants for children with developmental disorders and special healthcare needs whose medical expenses not covered, or not fully covered, by a family's commercial health insurance.

Website: https://www.uhccf.org

---

55 - Variety – The Children's Charity

Assists children with disabilities by providing medical equipment, therapy, and other services.

Website: https://www.variety.org

---

56 - Wheel to Walk Foundation

Specifically for individuals twenty years old or younger who live in Idaho, California, Washington, or Oregon, they could help you obtain medical & adaptive equipment or therapy services not provided by insurance that will improve quality of life. This may include gait trainers, wheelchairs, therapy tricycles, speech therapy, etc.

Website: https://www.wheeltowalk.com

---

57 - Williams Syndrome Association

Provides resources, advocacy, information and emotional support for individuals with Williams Syndrome and their families.

Website: https://williams-syndrome.org

In addition to the above information, in the United States, several lesser-known benefits and resources are available to individuals with disabilities and their families. These benefits vary according to location, so you need to investigate whether these options are available in your locale and advocate for your child's right to access them at reduced rates or free of cost.

Transportation and Travel

One such benefit is providing free or discounted travel for people with disabilities through various transportation programs.

Americans with Disabilities Act (ADA) Paratransit Services - Under the Americans with Disabilities Act (ADA) Paratransit Services, public transit agencies must provide paratransit services for individuals who cannot use fixed-route transit systems due to their disability. This service offers door-to-door transportation for eligible individuals at no additional cost.

Reduced Fare Programs - Many public transportation systems offer reduced fares for individuals with disabilities. These programs often provide significant discounts on fares for buses, trains, subways, and other forms of public transportation.

Accessible Parking Permits - People with disabilities may qualify for accessible parking permits, allowing them to park in designated accessible parking spaces closer to building entrances. These permits often have additional benefits, such as extended parking times or waived parking fees in certain areas.

Air Carrier Access Act (ACAA) Protections - Most airports have dedicated accessibility services teams trained to assist disabled passengers. These teams can provide guidance, support, and assistance throughout the airport journey, from check-in to boarding and disembarkation. The Air Carrier Access Act (ACAA) prohibits discrimination against individuals with disabilities in air travel. It requires airlines to provide accommodations, such as wheelchair assistance, accessible seating, and assistance with boarding and deplaning.

Amtrak Disability Travel Services - Airlines offer priority boarding for passengers with disabilities to ensure they have ample time to board the aircraft and settle into their seats comfortably. Priority boarding allows passengers with disabilities to board the plane before other passengers, reducing the stress and anxiety associated with the boarding process. Amtrak Disability Travel Services offers various services and accommodations for passengers with disabilities, including accessible seating, priority boarding, wheelchair assistance, and accessible restrooms on trains.

Accessible Transportation Vouchers - Some local governments and non-profit organizations provide transportation vouchers or subsidies to help offset the cost of transportation for individuals with disabilities. Some ride-sharing companies offer accessibility programs for individuals with disabilities, giving wheelchair-accessible vehicles and trained drivers to assist passengers with mobility needs.

Healthcare and Therapies

Medical Equipment Loan Programs - Some community organizations and non-profits operate medical equipment loan programs, providing families with access to essential medical equipment for their children with disabilities on a temporary basis. These programs allow families to borrow items such as wheelchairs, hospital beds, and adaptive seating at little to no cost.

Therapeutic Horseback Riding Programs - Therapeutic horseback riding programs offer children with disabilities the opportunity to engage in therapeutic activities involving horseback riding and equine-assisted therapy. These programs can provide physical, emotional, and cognitive benefits for children with disabilities while promoting social interaction and confidence-building.

Adaptive Sports and Recreation Programs - Adaptive Sports and Recreation Programs: Adaptive sports and recreation programs offer children with disabilities the chance to participate in various adaptive sports and recreational activities tailored to their abilities. These programs promote physical fitness, socialization, and teamwork while empowering children with disabilities to explore new interests and hobbies.

Local Government and Community Organisations

Home Modifications Grants - Some local governments and non-profit organizations offer grants or financial assistance programs to help families cover the cost of home modifications to accommodate a child with disabilities. These modifications may include installing ramps, widening doorways, or adding accessible bathrooms.

Respite Care Services - Respite care services provide temporary relief to caregivers of individuals with disabilities by offering short-term, supervised care for their children. These services allow caregivers to take a break from their caregiving responsibilities while ensuring their child receives proper care and support.

Technology Assistance Programs - Some organizations provide grants or loans to help families purchase assistive technology devices and equipment for their children with disabilities. These devices may include communication devices, mobility aids, or adaptive computer software.

Medical equipment loan programs - Some community organizations and non-profits operate medical equipment loan programs, providing families with access to essential medical equipment for their children with disabilities on a temporary basis. These programs allow families to borrow items such as wheelchairs, hospital beds, and adaptive seating at little to no cost.

Therapeutic Horseback Riding Programs - Therapeutic horseback riding programs offer children with disabilities the opportunity to engage in therapeutic activities involving horseback riding and equine-assisted therapy. These programs can provide physical, emotional, and cognitive benefits for children with disabilities while promoting social interaction and confidence-building.

Many camps and recreational programs offer scholarships or financial assistance to children with disabilities to enable them to participate in activities such as summer camps, sports programs, and arts and crafts.

Part 2 - Canada

"Really, at the end of the day, the only thing you can control is yourself; the only person you can truly educate is yourself. You have to redefine what beauty is to you so you can't be affected by what people are saying."

—*Rupi Kaur, Canadian Poet and Illustrator*

In Canada, numerous organizations provide special needs services, and these resources are readily accessible online. You might already know the benefits available under various Canadian government programs and initiatives:

❖ Provincial Ministries of Education: In Canada, each province/territory has its Ministry of Education responsible for overseeing education,

including services for students with special needs. For example, in Ontario, you can find information from the Ontario Ministry of Education.
https://www.ontario.ca/page/special-education-laws-and-policies

❖ Canada Pension Plan Disability (CPP-D): The Canada Pension Plan Disability provides financial assistance to individuals with severe and prolonged disabilities. It's a valuable resource for families working through the challenges of supporting a child with special needs.
https://www.canada.ca/en/services/benefits/publicpensions/cpp/cpp-disability-benefit.html

❖ Disability Tax Credit (DTC): Families caring for a child with a severe and prolonged impairment may qualify for the Disability Tax Credit, providing them with financial relief through reduced income tax.
https://www.canada.ca/en/revenue-agency/services/tax/individuals/segments/tax-credits-deductions-persons-disabilities/disability-tax-credit/eligible-dtc.html

❖ This organization specializes in supporting families new to Canada. It shares information on various benefits and credits available for persons with disabilities and their caregivers - an invaluable resource.
https://kidsnewtocanada.ca/uploads/documents/Outreach_Factsheet_PersonswithDisabilities_EW_2022-01-25_EN.pdf

If these are unfamiliar to you, taking the time to explore how your child could benefit from these mainstream sources of support is recommended. Numerous reliable articles and guidance are available online to assist with the application process. It's crucial to note that procedures may vary across provinces and territories.

Canada

In the following section, I share information on lesser-known, inconspicuous sources of support that you may be able to access if your child resides in Canada.

---

1 - Ability Online

Offers a safe online community for children and youth with disabilities to connect and access resources.

Website: https://www.abilityonline.org

---

2 - ALS Society of Canada

Supports care, funding research and spreading awareness of ALS.

Website: https://als.ca

---

3 - Angel Hair for Kids

Offers free wigs and hair systems to children in Canada who have lost their hair due to medical conditions or treatments.

Website: https://www.acvf.ca/angel-hair-for-kids

---

4 - Angelman Syndrome Foundation

Provides resources, support, and advocacy for individuals with Angelman Syndrome and their families.

Website: https://www.angelman.org

---

5 - Assistance for Children with Severe Disabilities (ACSD)

Provides financial assistance to families of children with severe disabilities to help cover the costs of disability-related expenses.

Website: https://www.mcss.gov.on.ca/en/mcss/programs/social/odsp/child.aspx

---

6 - Autism in Mind (AIM)

Provides support and professional services such as communication, social and learning skills programs for children and youth with autism.

Website: https://autisminmind.org

---

7 - Autism Speaks Canada

Provides resources, advocacy, and support for individuals with autism spectrum disorder and their families.

Website: https://www.autismspeaks.ca

---

8 - BC Elks Association

Provide camping facilities for underprivileged, disabled and special needs children as well as other groups of children who would not otherwise be able to attend a camp.

Website: https://sites.google.com/site/bcelksassociation/home

---

9 - Blind Beginnings

Their mission is to inspire children and youth who are blind or partially sighted and their families through diverse programs, experiences, counselling and peer support, and opportunities to create fulfilling lives.

Website: https://www.blindbeginnings.ca

---

10 - Canada's National Ballet School

Their NBS Kids – Adaptive Dance Program offers adapted creative movement classes for children aged four and over with diverse cognitive, physical and developmental needs.

Website: https://www.nbs-enb.ca

---

11 - Canadian Association for Williams Syndrome

Provides support, education, and advocacy for individuals with Williams syndrome and their families.

Website: https://www.williamssyndrome.ca

---

12 - Canadian Disability Resources Society

Provides a comprehensive directory of businesses and organizations offering accessible resources, products and services for the disabled community.

Website: https://www.disabilityresources.ca/home

---

13 - Canadian Down Syndrome Society (CDSS)

Offers resources, advocacy, and support for individuals with Down syndrome and their families.

Website: https://cdss.ca

14 - Canadian Hard of Hearing Association (CHHA)

Offers support, advocacy, and resources for children and individuals with hearing loss or deafness.

Website: https://www.chha.ca

---

15 - Canadian Hearing Society

Provides support, communication devices, and resources for children with hearing loss or deafness.

Website: https://www.chs.ca

---

16 - Canadian National Institute for the Blind (CNIB)

Offers services, programs, and support for children with visual impairments and their families.

Website: https://cnib.ca/en

---

17 - Communication Assistance for Youth and Adults (CAYA)

Supports adults aged 19 years and older who require an augmentative/alternative communication (AAC) system due to a severe communication disability.

Website: https://cayabc.net

---

18 - Child Development Institute

Provides a range of services, including assessments, therapies, and support for children with developmental disabilities.

Website: https://childdevelop.ca

---

19 - Childhood Cancer Canada Foundation

Offers support programs and financial assistance to families of children with cancer, including medical expenses, transportation, and accommodation.

Website: https://www.childhoodcancer.ca

---

20 - Children's Ability Fund

Offers financial assistance for mobility equipment, assistive technology and programs for children with disabilities.

Website: https://childrensabilityfund.ca

---

21 - Children's Rehabilitation Foundation

Provides funding for therapy, equipment, and other support such as specialized communication resources for children with disabilities.

Website: https://www.crf.mb.ca

---

22 - Children's Treatment Network

Coordinates programs and services to support children and youth with multiple special needs.

Website: https://www.ctnsy.ca

---

23 - CNIB Foundation

Provides innovative programs such as employment workshops, recreational activities, peer support groups or technology training to Canadians affected by vision loss.

Website: https://www.cnib.ca/en?region=on

---

24 - Disabled Sailing Association of Ontario

Provides accessible sailing programs and opportunities for individuals with disabilities.

Website: https://disabledsailingontario.com

25 - Easter Seals Canada

Offers financial assistance for children and adults with disabilities in several areas including assistive and adaptive technology, specialized education and training programs and sports, recreation and leisure programs.

Website: https://www.easterseals.ca

---

26 - Epilepsy Ontario

Provides resources, advocacy, and support services for children and families affected by epilepsy.

Website: https://epilepsyontario.org

---

27 - International Rett Syndrome Foundation

Provides resources, research funding, and support for individuals with Rett Syndrome and their families.

Website: https://www.rettsyndrome.org

---

28 - Jake's House for Children with Autism

Offers programs such as Jake's House Skills Development Training Program & Industry Training Programs along with an inclusive housing program for individuals and families living with autism.

Website: https://www.jakeshouse.ca

---

29 - Jumpstart Charities

Offers programs such as Jake's House Skills Development Training Program & Industry Training Programs along with an inclusive housing program for individuals living with autism.

Website: https://www.jakeshouse.ca

---

30 - Kids Upfront Foundation

Distributes tickets to arts, culture, and sports events to children facing various challenges, including disabilities.

Website: https://www.kidsupfront.com

---

31 - Learning Disabilities Association of Canada (LDAC)

Provides advocacy, assessments, tools, resources and information for people with learning disabilities and their families.

Website: https://www.ldac-acta.ca

32   -   Lions Foundation of Canada Dog Guides

Offers guide dogs and other service animals to children with disabilities to enhance their Independence and mobility.

Website: https://www.dogguides.com

33   -   Make-A-Wish Canada

Works with the community to provide children living with high-risk, life threatening illnesses the opportunity to realize their most heartfelt wish.

Website: https://makeawish.ca.

34   -   Muscular Dystrophy Canada

Provides support, resources, and financial assistance through the Community Services Fund for children with muscular dystrophy and neuromuscular disorders.

Website: https://muscle.ca

35   -   Neil Squire Society

Offers funding and several free programs in various areas, such as employment, computer tutoring, and assistive technology, to empower Canadians with disabilities.

Canada

Website: https://www.neilsquire.ca

---

36 - Reach Canada

Assists individuals with disabilities in dealing with legal issues and provides resources for inclusion.

Website: https://www.reach.ca

---

37 - Rick Hansen Foundation

Supports initiatives that improve accessibility and inclusivity for people with disabilities.

Website: https://www.rickhansen.com

---

38 - Sensity Deafblind and Sensory Support Network of Canada

Provides services, equipment, and support for children who are deafblind or have sensory impairments.

Website: https://www.sensity.ca

---

39 - Sunshine Dreams for Kids

Grants wishes and provides dream experiences for children with severe physical disabilities or life-threatening illnesses.

Website: https://sunshine.ca

40 - Tetra Society of North America

They fund the design and building of assistive devices that are custom-made for disabled individuals that are either not available commercially or cost-prohibitive providing greater independence, quality of life, and inclusion.

Website: https://tetrasociety.org

41 - The Association of Parent Support Groups (APSGO)

Helps parents, guardians, grandparents, stepparents or any adult concerned about the behaviour of young person who is struggling emotionally, withdrawn, acting out, using drugs or alcohol, exhibiting aggressive behavior, missing school or in conflict with the law.

Website: https://apsgo.ca/about-us

In Canada, children with special needs and disabilities may also have access to several additional lesser-known benefits and services that can help alleviate some of the financial burdens associated with their condition. These vary according to location. Some examples these variable benefits are listed below.

Travel

Free or discounted travel - Many cities and municipalities in Canada offer free or discounted public transit fares for individuals with disabilities. These reduced fares may apply to buses, trains, subways, and other forms of public transportation. Eligibility criteria and application processes may vary depending on the transit authority. Some transportation providers offer companion fares for individuals with disabilities who require assistance while traveling. These companion fares allow the disabled person to bring a companion or caregiver along at a reduced or no cost, depending on the provider's policy.

Accessible Transportation Services - In addition to public transit, some regions in Canada provide specialized accessible transportation services for individuals with disabilities who cannot use conventional public transit due to their mobility limitations. These services may include accessible vans, buses, or taxis equipped with ramps or lifts to accommodate wheelchair users.

Access to Air Travel Assistance - Some airlines provide assistance and accommodations to passengers with disabilities under the Canadian Transportation Agency's Accessible Transportation for Persons with Disabilities Regulations. This assistance may include priority boarding, assistance with stowing mobility aids, and support with navigating the airport terminal.

Government Travel Assistance Programs - Some provincial and territorial governments in Canada offer travel assistance programs for individuals with disabilities who need to travel for medical purposes or specialized treatments. These programs may provide financial assistance to help cover the cost of transportation, accommodations, and other related expenses.

Ferry Travel Discounts - In regions where ferry travel is a primary mode of transportation, such as coastal areas and remote communities, ferry operators may offer discounts or exemptions for individuals with disabilities and their companions. These discounts can help make ferry travel more affordable and accessible for people with disabilities.

Taxi Subsidy Programs - Some municipalities in Canada operate taxi subsidy programs for individuals with disabilities who are unable to use conventional public transit due to their mobility impairments. These programs provide subsidies or vouchers to offset the cost of taxi fares for eligible individuals.

Sport and Leisure Services

Accessible Summer Camps - Many summer camps across Canada offer specialized programs and accommodations for children with disabilities. These camps provide various activities, including outdoor adventures, arts and crafts, sports, and team-building exercises, all adapted to meet the needs and abilities of children with diverse disabilities.

Adaptive Sports Programs - Adaptive sports programs offer children with disabilities the opportunity to participate in various sports and recreational activities tailored to their abilities. These programs may include wheelchair basketball, sled hockey, adaptive skiing, swimming, and track and field events.

Therapeutic Riding Programs - In certain regions, there are free or subsidized therapeutic riding programs for children with disabilities. These programs offer physical, emotional, and cognitive benefits while promoting confidence, independence, and social interaction.

Accessible Parks and Playgrounds - Many communities in Canada have accessible parks and playgrounds equipped with features such as wheelchair-accessible swings, sensory-friendly play areas, and inclusive play structures designed to accommodate children with disabilities. These parks provide opportunities for children to play and interact with their peers in an inclusive environment.

Arts and Cultural Programs - Arts and cultural organizations often offer subsidized or free programs and workshops for children with disabilities to explore their creative interests and talents. These programs may include art classes, music therapy sessions, drama workshops, and sensory-friendly performances tailored to the needs of children with diverse disabilities.

Community Recreation Centers - Community recreation centers may offer subsidized or free recreational programs and activities for children with disabilities, such as swimming lessons, dance classes, martial arts, and fitness programs. These programs allow children to stay active, learn new skills, and socialize with their peers in a supportive environment.

Accessible Outdoor Adventures - Some organizations and tour operators in Canada offer subsidized or free outdoor adventure programs for children with disabilities, including adaptive hiking, camping, canoeing, and nature exploration activities. These programs allow children to experience the beauty of nature and develop confidence and resilience in an outdoor setting.

Healthcare

Specialized Pediatric Care - Children with disabilities may require specialized medical care from pediatric specialists, such as developmental pediatricians, neurologists, orthopedic surgeons, and rehabilitation therapists. These services are typically covered under the publicly-funded healthcare system and may be provided free of charge or at a reduced cost to families.

Assistive Devices and Equipment - Children with disabilities may require assistive devices and equipment to support their mobility, communication, and activities of daily living. In some provinces and territories, government-funded programs provide financial assistance or subsidies to help families cover the cost of assistive devices such as wheelchairs, communication devices, orthotics, and hearing aids.

Therapeutic Services - Children with disabilities may benefit from various therapeutic services, including physiotherapy, occupational therapy, speech-language therapy, and behavioral therapy. These services are often covered under provincial healthcare plans or may be available through government-funded programs for children with special needs.

Prescription Medications - Prescription medications prescribed to manage the symptoms of a child's disability or underlying medical condition may be covered under provincial drug benefit programs or through private insurance plans. Some provinces also offer special drug programs for children with disabilities that provide coverage for medications not included in standard formularies.

Home Nursing Care - Children with complex medical needs or disabilities that require ongoing medical care may be eligible for home nursing care services provided by publicly-funded healthcare programs. These services may include skilled nursing care, personal care assistance, medication administration, and medical monitoring delivered in the child's home environment.

Medical Transportation Services - Children with disabilities who require specialized medical treatments or appointments may be eligible for subsidized or free medical transportation services provided by provincial healthcare programs. These services help ensure that children can access necessary medical care, even living in remote or underserved areas.

Respite Care Services - Respite care services provide temporary relief to caregivers of children with disabilities by offering short-term, supervised care for their children. Some provinces and territories offer publicly-funded respite care programs that provide eligible families with free or subsidized respite care services.

By taking advantage of these lesser-known benefits and services, children with special needs and disabilities in Canada can access affordable and accessible services and amenities that support their mobility, health and welfare. I encourage you to research these programs and resources to maximize the support the support available to your family.

Part 3 - The United Kingdom

"Trees bear fruit, fruits have seeds, seeds hold trees. Everyone, indeed everything has something to offer in the cycle of life."

— *Andrea Campbell, Author & Linguist*

In the United Kingdom, several organizations provide services for individuals with special needs, and these resources are conveniently displayed online. You may already know the benefits available under various UK government programs and initiatives.

- ❖ Department for Education (DfE) and Special Educational Needs and Disability (SEND) Unit: In the UK, the Department for Education oversees education policies related to special educational needs and disabilities. The SEND Unit ensures access to quality education for children and young people with special educational needs and disabilities. Please contact them at: https://www.gov.uk/children-with-special-educational-needs/special-educational-needs-support.

- ❖ UK Government Disability Living Allowance (DLA) and Personal Independence Payment (PIP) - Families in the UK caring for a child with a disability may be eligible for financial support through Disability Living Allowance or Personal Independence Payment. You may qualify for Carer's Allowance if you provide substantial care for a child with special needs. See https://www.gov.uk/browse/disabilities/benefits.

- ❖ As in the USA and Canada, various non-governmental organizations in the UK provide information to families caring for children with special needs and disabilities. They include Scope (https://www.scope.org.uk/), Family

Action UK (https://www.family-action.org.uk), and Mencap (https://www.mencap.org.uk).

If the above organizations are unfamiliar to you, it's beneficial to explore how your child could benefit from these mainstream sources of support. Numerous reliable articles and guidance are available online to assist with the application process.

In this section, I shed light on lesser-known, inconspicuous sources of support that you may be able to access if your child resides in the United Kingdom.

1 - ADHD Foundation

Offers support, information, and resources for individuals with attention deficit hyperactivity disorder (ADHD) and their families.

Website: https://www.adhdfoundation.org.uk

---

2 - Action for Kids

Provides mobility equipment, work placements, and support services for disabled children and young people.

Website: https://www.actionforkids.org

---

3 - Action Duchenne

Offers support and resources for families affected by Duchenne muscular dystrophy.

Website: https:// www.actionduchenne.org

---

4 - Bibic

Offers practical support and therapy for children and young people with developmental and neurological difficulties or disabilities.

Website: https://www.bibic.org.uk

5 - Bobath Centre for Children with Cerebral Palsy

Offers specialist therapy and support for children with cerebral palsy and their families.

Website: https://www.bobath.org.uk

---

6 - Boparan Charitable Trust

Offers financial assistance for disabled children's medical treatment, equipment, and therapies.

Website: https://www.theboparancharitabletrust.com

---

7 - Brain Injury Rehabilitation Trust

Provides specialist residential rehabilitation and support services for children and adults with acquired brain injury.

Website: https://www.thedtgroup.org/brain-injury

---

8 - Brainwave

A charity that exists to help children with disabilities and additional needs to achieve greater independence by aiming to improve mobility, communication skills and learning potential through a range of specialist therapies.

Website: https://www.brainwave.org.uk

---

9 - Caudwell Children

Provides support, grants, and therapy services for disabled children and their families.

Website: https://www.caudwellchildren.com

---

10 - Cerebra Charity

Provides support, information, and resources for children with brain conditions and their families.

Website: https://www.cerebra.org.uk

11 - Child Brain Injury Trust

Offers support, information, and resources for children with acquired brain injury and their families.

Website: https://childbraininjurytrust.org.uk

---

12 - Children Today Charitable Trust

Assists in funding specialized equipment and services for children and young people with disabilities.

Website: https://www.childrentoday.org.uk

13 - Children's Heart Federation

Provides information, support, and resources for families of children with heart conditions.

Website: https://www.chfed.org.uk

---

14 - Contact

Offers a helpline, support groups, and information for families with disabled children, covering various disabilities and conditions.

Website: https://www.contact.org.uk

---

15 - Daisy Chain Project

Offers a range of support services, including respite care, activity clubs, and parent support, for families of children with autism.

Website: https://www.daisychainproject.co.uk

---

16 - Deafblind UK

Provides support, information, and resources for individuals who are deafblind.

Website: https://www.deafblind.org.uk

17 - Disabled Children's Partnership

Offers resources, information, and access to grants for families of disabled children.

Website: https://www.disabledchildrenspartnership.org.uk

---

18 - Disabled Living Foundation

Offers information, advice, and guidance on equipment and independent living for disabled children and adults.

Website: https://www.dlf.org.uk

---

19 - Down's Syndrome Association

Provides information, support, and resources for individuals with Down's syndrome and their families.

Website: https://www.downs-syndrome.org.uk

---

20 - Down's Syndrome Research Foundation

Supports research, education, and advocacy for individuals with Down's syndrome.

Website: https://www.dsrf-uk.org

21 - Dyspraxia Foundation

Provides support, information, and resources for individuals with dyspraxia and their families.

Website: https://dyspraxiafoundation.org.uk

---

22 - Elizabeth Foundation

Provides support and education for deaf children and their families.

Website: https://elizabeth-foundation.org

---

23 - Family Action

Offers financial support, grants, and advocacy services for families with disabled children.

Website: https://www.family-action.org.uk

---

24 - Family Fund

Offers grants for essential items, family breaks, and other needs of low-income families raising disabled children.

Website: https://www.familyfund.org.uk

---

25 - Footprints Conductive Education Centre

Offers conductive education programs for children with motor disorders, helping them develop their physical and social skills.

Website: https://www.footprintscec.org

---

26 - Fragile X Society

Provides support, information, and resources for individuals and families affected by Fragile X syndrome.

Website: https://www.fragilex.org.uk

---

27 - Genetic Alliance UK

Offers support, information, and advocacy for individuals and families affected by genetic disorders.

Website: https://geneticalliance.org.uk

---

28 - Kids

Provides a wide range of services nationally for disabled children, young people and their families. Services cover three main areas: information, advice & family support; play and social; and learning and development.

Website: https://www.kids.org.uk

29 - Kids Cancer Charity

Offers financial support, therapies, and respite care for children with cancer and their families.

Website: https://www.kidscancercharity.org

---

30 - KidsOut

Organises fun days out, toys, and play equipment for children with disabilities, including those in refuge homes or with limited resources.

Website: https://www.kidsout.org.uk

---

31 - Limb Power

Support amputees, individuals with limb difference and their families to bridge the gap between hospital rehabilitation and community and school engagement to rebuild lives and improve physical, social and mental well-being. Promotes and enables physical activity and sport for individuals with limb impairments.

Website: https://www.limbpower.com

---

32 - Makaton Charity

Provides training and resources for using Makaton, a communication system for individuals with communication difficulties.

Website: https://www.makaton.org

---

33 - Merlin's Magic Wand

Grants magical experiences and special treats to children with life-limiting illnesses or significant disabilities.

Website: https://www.merlinsmagicwand.org

---

34 - Muscular Dystrophy UK

Provides support, information, and advocacy for individuals with muscular dystrophy.

Website: https://www.musculardystrophyuk.org

---

35 - Music as Therapy International

Uses music therapy to improve the lives of children with disabilities and additional needs.

Website: https://www.musicastherapy.org

---

36 - National Autistic Society

Offers support, information, and advocacy for individuals with autism spectrum disorders.

Website: https://www.autism.org.uk

37 - National Deaf Children's Society

Offers support, information, and resources for deaf children and their families.

Website: https://www.ndcs.org.uk

---

38 - Newlife Foundation for Disabled Children

Offers grants for equipment, emergency support, and play therapy for disabled children.

Website: https://www.newlifecharity.co.uk

---

39 - Rainbows Children's Hospice

Offers care, support, and respite services for children with life-limiting conditions and their families.

Website: https://www.rainbows.co.uk

---

40 - Rainbow Trust Children's Charity

Offers emotional and practical support for families with a seriously ill child, including sibling support.

Website: https://www.rainbowtrust.org.uk

41 - Rare Chromosome Disorder Support Group

Provides support and information for families affected by rare chromosome disorders.

Website: https://www.rarechromo.org

---

42 - Rett UK

Supports individuals with Rett syndrome and their families through information, guidance, and access to specialist services.

Website: https://www.rettuk.org

---

43 - RDA

Provides therapeutic horse riding and carriage driving activities for children and adults with disabilities to improve their physical and emotional well-being.

Website: https://www.rda.org.uk

---

44 - Sense

Supports children and adults with complex disabilities through specialist services, including Communication support, sensory play, and respite care.

Website: https://www.sense.org.uk

45 - Small Steps

Provides intensive physiotherapy sessions and support for children with children aged birth to 5 years who have cerebral palsy or other forms of motor impairment, syndromes or sensory impairment.

Website: https://www.smallsteps.org.uk

46 - Smith-Magenis Syndrome Foundation UK

Offers support and information for individuals and families affected by Smith-Magenis Syndrome.

Website: https://www.smith-magenis.co.uk

47 - Special Kids in the UK

Offers support, advice, and information for families of children with special needs, including a supportive online community.

Website: https://www.specialkidsintheuk.org

48 - Spinal Muscular Atrophy UK

Provides information, support, and advocacy for individuals with spinal muscular atrophy and their families.

Website: https://smauk.org.uk

---

49 - Stick 'n' Step

Provides conductive education, support, and therapy for children with cerebral palsy.

Website: https://www.sticknstep.org

---

50 - Sycamore Trust UK

Offers support and resources for families of children with autistic spectrum disorders.

Website: https://www.sycamoretrust.org.uk

---

51 - The Children's Trust

Provides rehabilitation, support, and care for children with brain injury and complex disabilities.

Website: https://www.thechildrenstrust.org.uk

---

52 - Theodora Children's Charity

Sends "Giggle Doctors" to hospitals, hospices, and specialist care centres to bring joy and laughter to sick and disabled children.

Website: https://www.theodora.org.uk

53 - Together for Short Lives

Provides support, information, and advocacy for children with life-threatening and life-limiting conditions.

Website: https://www.togetherforshortlives.org.uk

---

54 - Tourettes Action

Provides information, support, and advocacy for individuals and families affected by Tourette syndrome.

Website: https://www.tourettes-action.org.uk

---

55 - Tree of Hope

Assists families in raising funds for treatment, therapies, and equipment for disabled children.

Website: https://www.treeofhope.org.uk

---

56 - Variety – the Children's Charity

Provides grants for equipment, therapies, and memorable experiences to improve the lives of children with special needs.

Website: https://www.variety.org.uk

57 - WellChild

Offers practical and emotional support to seriously ill children and their families, including respite care, home adaptations, and nursing support.

Website: https://www.wellchild.org.uk

---

58 - Whizz-Kidz

Provides mobility equipment, wheelchair training, and opportunities for disabled children and young people to participate in various activities.

Website: https://www.whizz-kidz.org.uk

---

59 - Young Epilepsy

Provides information, training, and support for children and young people with epilepsy and their families.

Website: https://www.youngepilepsy.org.uk

In the United Kingdom, individuals with disabilities may have access to other lesser-known benefits and services. Some of these benefits vary according to location, so you need to investigate whether they are available in your locale, and advocate for your child's right to access them at reduced rates or free of cost.

Free or Discounted Travel

Disabled Persons Railcard - The Disabled Persons Railcard offers discounted train travel for individuals with disabilities and their companions. Holders of the railcard are entitled to one-third off most rail fares across Great Britain, making it more affordable to travel by train for leisure, work, or medical appointments.

Blue Badge Scheme - The Blue Badge Scheme provides parking concessions for people with severe mobility impairments who have difficulty walking or navigating public transport. Blue Badge holders are entitled to park in designated accessible parking spaces, often free of charge or at a reduced rate, in on-street parking and car parks across the UK.

Taxicard Scheme - The Taxicard Scheme offers subsidized taxi fares for individuals with mobility impairments who cannot use public transport independently. Eligible individuals receive a subsidy towards the cost of taxi journeys within their local area, providing greater accessibility and flexibility in transportation options.

Community Transport Services - Many local authorities and charitable organizations operate community transport services for individuals with disabilities who face barriers to using public transport. These services may include accessible minibuses, dial-a-ride services, and volunteer drivers, offering door-to-door transportation for essential trips and social outings.

National Concessionary Travel Scheme - The National Concessionary Travel Scheme provides free or discounted bus travel for individuals with disabilities across England, Scotland, and Wales. Eligible individuals receive a concessionary travel pass, allowing them to travel on local bus services free of charge or at a reduced fare.

Motability Scheme - The Motability Scheme enables individuals with disabilities to lease a car, scooter, or powered wheelchair using their mobility allowance. Participants in the scheme receive a fully comprehensive insurance package, servicing and maintenance, and breakdown assistance, providing greater independence and mobility for disabled individuals and their families.

Disabled Students' Allowance - Disabled students attending higher education institutions in the UK may be eligible for the Disabled Students' Allowance (DSA). This allowance provides financial support to cover additional costs associated with disability-related needs, including travel to and from university or college campuses. DSA funding can help cover travel expenses, such as transport passes, mileage reimbursement, or specialized transportation services, ensuring disabled students can access their educational opportunities.

Air Travel Support

Priority Boarding - Airlines often provide priority boarding for passengers with disabilities, including children, allowing them to board the aircraft before other passengers. Priority boarding helps reduce stress and anxiety for children with disabilities and their families by providing extra time to settle into their seats and stow their belongings.

Assistance with Mobility - Children with mobility impairments or physical disabilities may require assistance navigating the airport terminal and boarding the aircraft. Airports offer wheelchair assistance and escort services to help disabled children safely move through the airport. Airlines also provide onboard wheelchairs to assist passengers with mobility challenges during the flight.

Special Seating Arrangements - Airlines accommodate children with disabilities by providing special seating arrangements to meet their needs. This may include bulkhead seating with extra legroom, seats with movable armrests, or seats near the aircraft's lavatories for easy access. Airlines strive to accommodate seating preferences and medical requirements to ensure the child's comfort and safety during the flight.

In-flight Assistance - Flight attendants receive training to assist and support passengers with disabilities, including children, throughout the flight. They can help with meal service, access the lavatory, and move about the aircraft. Flight attendants are sensitive to the needs of children with disabilities and strive to make their flight experience as comfortable as possible.

Special Meals and Dietary Requirements - Airlines offer special meal options to accommodate dietary restrictions and medical needs, including allergies, food intolerances, and dietary preferences. Parents can request special meals for their child with disabilities when booking their flight, ensuring their nutritional needs are met during the journey.

Assistance Animals - Children with disabilities who require the assistance of service animals, such as guide dogs or emotional support animals, are welcome to travel with their animal companions on many airlines. Airlines have policies and procedures to accommodate service animals and ensure their well-being during the flight.

Health and Wellness

Range of therapies - In addition to the more common physiotherapy, occupational therapy, and speech therapy, children with disabilities may be able to access play therapy, music and art therapy, behavioral therapy, and animal-assisted therapy.

Sensory Rooms – These are specially designed spaces with various sensory equipment and materials, such as interactive lighting, tactile surfaces, soothing sounds, and fragrances. These rooms provide a calming and stimulating environment for children with sensory processing disorders or developmental disabilities to explore and engage their senses in a safe and controlled setting.

Accessible Adventure Playgrounds - Inclusive play structures and equipment designed to accommodate children of all abilities, including those with physical disabilities, sensory impairments, and mobility challenges. These playgrounds offer opportunities for disabled children to play, climb, swing, and explore alongside their peers in an inclusive and supportive environment.

Therapeutic Gardens – These are outdoor spaces designed to promote relaxation, sensory stimulation, and therapeutic activities for individuals with disabilities. These gardens may include features such as wheelchair-accessible pathways, raised planters for gardening activities, sensory plants, water features, and quiet seating areas, providing a tranquil and therapeutic retreat for disabled children and their families.

Accessible Sports Facilities - These facilities offer adapted sports and recreational activities tailored to the needs of disabled children, including wheelchair sports, adaptive swimming, sensory-friendly fitness classes, and inclusive team sports.

Multi-Sensory Storytelling Sessions - Multi-sensory storytelling sessions combine storytelling with interactive sensory experiences to engage children with disabilities in literacy and communication activities.

These sessions may incorporate tactile props, sound effects, music, and movement to enhance the storytelling experience and make it accessible to children with diverse abilities and learning styles.

Accessible Outdoor and Indoor Cinema Screenings - These screenings offer inclusive movie-watching experiences for disabled children and their families featuring open-air screenings with wheelchair-accessible seating areas, captioning or subtitles, and sensory-friendly adjustments such as reduced lighting and sound levels.

By accessing these lesser-known benefits and services, children with disabilities in the UK can enjoy greater accessibility, independence, and participation in everyday activities. Please explore and inquire about available amenities and opportunities for recreation, socialization, and personal growth that cater to your child's unique needs and interests.

In your research, you will likely find accessible activities and discover hidden gems that can enrich your child's life and create memorable experiences for the whole family.

International Grants

Discovering international grants to support the development of children with special needs can be a valuable endeavor for families seeking additional resources and assistance. There are many grant-giving websites, and some organizations operate in multiple countries. One such web page that is worth exploring is https://international.grantwatch.com/cat/7/disabilities-grants.html/2.

In many instances, these grants are not directly accessible by individual families, but they are available to fund initiatives and programs that ultimately benefit children with disabilities. To leverage these opportunities, please contact your local charitable organizations, support workers, medical professionals, or other relevant organizations and personnel to explore the possibility of applying.

International Grants

The procedure for securing international grants for individual families is more complex, but applying via a local entity can streamline the application process and increase the likelihood of success.

By collaborating with knowledgeable professionals and advocates, families can navigate the complexities of international grant applications in order to access the support they need to enhance their child's development and well-being. If the professionals are unaware of the opportunities, this is your chance to create awareness so that your child and other children in your community can access the help they need.

So, while international grants may primarily target organizations, don't be daunted by the challenge. Keep the goal at the forefront of your thoughts, and don't hesitate to pursue the opportunities to explore these potential sources of support.

Conclusion

Caring for a child with special needs is a journey of profound depth, one marked by both the inherent rewards and the occasional challenges that punctuate the role of parenthood. Within these pages, I have offered information and a source of empowerment for families on this unique path.

As your child strides towards adulthood, the challenges and triumphs evolve. This booklet serves as a steadfast companion, providing guidance on crucial sources of aid as you support your child toward a life rich in fulfillment and independence. And though you may feel like you are on a lonely road, remember that a robust support system, fortified by information and resources, is a cornerstone for overcoming the intricate terrain of special needs parenting.

Throughout this book, we have uncovered several hidden treasures that can positively impact the lives of

Conclusion

children with disabilities and their caregivers. Use this text not merely as a guide, but as a tool—an ally in your pursuit of the optimal care and support for your child. I hope the book has illuminated a world of untapped grants, resources, provisions, and amenities available to families across the United Kingdom, the United States, and Canada.

From little-known government programs and financial assistance to specialized therapies, recreational opportunities, and community amenities, the support package for children with special needs is rich and diverse. By shedding light on these lesser-known resources, this book has empowered families with the knowledge and tools needed to negotiate the complex terrain of disability support networks.

Consider this booklet as your compass, guiding you to organizations ready to lend a helping hand. It is a foundation, but as no one lives in a foundation, you must build on the knowledge and constantly pursue information to help you take positive steps as you face

Conclusion

the distinctive challenges and joys of caring for a child with special needs.

As we reflect on the journey of discovery undertaken in these pages, it is clear that the path to empowerment and inclusion is dotted with hidden gems waiting to be unearthed. By harnessing the power of these obscure benefits and provisions, your family can access the assistance, services, and amenities that enrich your child's life and enhance their sense of belonging and well-being.

But our journey does not end here. As we step forward into the future, let us continue to seek out and champion the services and benefits that make a world of difference for our children. Please share this information with others so that we, as parents of children with disabilities, can build a community that celebrates the unique abilities and potential inherent in all our children.

Conclusion

By sharing knowledge, fostering support networks, and advocating for understanding, we contribute to a world where children everywhere, irrespective of their abilities, are celebrated and allowed to thrive. Together, let us build a more inclusive and supportive society where every child can reach their full potential, regardless of their abilities or challenges.

Please Leave a Review

If you have enjoyed this book, I'd appreciate it if you'd leave me a review.

As independently published authors, reviews are essential. They promote the visibility of our books to other parents and caregivers so they, too, may access the information.

Thank you.

Resources

Admin, S. (2023, August 2). Government Programs for Children with Disabilities. Special Needs Alliance. https://www.specialneedsalliance.org/blog/government-programs-for-children-with-disabilities/

Benefits and credits available for persons with disabilities and their caregivers. (n.d.). KidsNewtoCanada.ca. Retrieved January 24, 2024, from https://kidsnewtocanada.ca/uploads/documents/Outreach_Factsheet_PersonswithDisabilities_EW_2022-01-25_EN.pdf

Benefits and financial help - GOV.UK. (n.d.). https://www.gov.uk/browse/disabilities/benefits

Canada Revenue Agency. (2024, January 23). Who is eligible - Disability tax credit (DTC). Canada.ca. https://www.canada.ca/en/revenue-agency/services/tax/individuals/segments/tax-credits-deductions-persons-disabilities/disability-tax-credit/eligible-dtc.html

Disability | SSA. (n.d.-c). https://www.ssa.gov/disability

Government Digital Service. (2014, November 25). Children with special educational needs and disabilities (SEND). GOV.UK. https://www.gov.uk/children-with-special-educational-needs/special-educational-needs-support

Service Canada. (2024, January 22). Canada Pension Plan disability benefits: Overview. Canada.ca. https://www.canada.ca/en/services/benefits/publicpensions/cpp/cpp-disability-benefit.html

Special education laws and policies. (n.d.). ontario.ca. https://www.ontario.ca/page/special-education-laws-and-policies

SSDI and SSI benefits for people with disabilities | USAGov. (n.d.). https://www.usa.gov/social-security-disability

Travel by air | Assistance dog travel guide. (n.d.). Guide Dogs Site. https://www.guidedogs.org.uk/getting-support/information-and-advice/travelling-with-your-assistance-dog/travel-by-air

US Department of Education (ED). (n.d.-b). OSEP: About OSEP. https://www2.ed.gov/about/offices/list/osers/osep/about.html

About the Author

 Andrea Campbell, MBA, MA, is a social entrepreneur, linguist, and author. Since publishing her first book in 2010, Andrea has released several inspirational, special needs parenting, business, and cultural books. Over the years, she has focused on supporting vulnerable people through education and inspiration.

As the mother of a child with special educational needs, she is particularly keen on working with families to enable their disabled children to aspire higher and achieve their potential. She is also the inventor of the Pocket Learner – a set of innovative educational resources for parents, caregivers, and educators of children with special educational needs.

Andrea also published several inspirational books, coloring books, journals, and activity books to inspire people everywhere. She resides with her family in London, UK, where she continues to have a positive impact through her writing, creative exploits, training programs, coaching, philanthropy, and inspirational speaking.

https://www.linkedin.com/in/andreacampbell6806
https://andreacampbell.co.uk
https://twitter.com/camptys

Other Books by the Author

The Blended Family Parenting Kids with Special Needs / Blended and Special

The 9-L model illustrated in "Blended and Special" explores the dynamics of stepfamilies caring for children with special needs and disabilities and presents the information in digestible nuggets ready for consumption by quintessential blended families juggling the demands of parenthood with caring for children with special needs.

Please note that the paperback of this book is called "Blended and Special." For technical reasons, the e-book version had to be renamed "The Blended Family Parenting Kids with Special Needs." Both books contain the same information.

Blended Family - A Guide for Stepparents

This book outlines seven attitudes that seriously harm blended families, including those caring for children with special needs and disabilities. This succinct book gets straight to the point and is easy to read and follow.

A Parent's Guide to Empowering Children with Special Needs

With 101 proven tips, this book covers many topics, including communication, behavior management, sensory integration, and fostering independence. The guide recognizes the challenges faced by parents and offers practical solutions to overcome them.

With chapters dedicated to self-care, managing daily routines, and enhancing academic success, you'll find the guidance you need to balance your well-being with that of your child.

The Pocket Learner Special Needs Education

The structure is built on six principles represented by the acronyms HOPE, FAITH, GENTLE(ness), JOY, LOVE, and PEACE. The framework revolves around the child - the star and fruit of the womb endowed with innate abilities and gifts.

The toolkit covers the range of roles, responsibilities, and activities that families and other relevant parties must implement. It advocates early and consistent intervention by the relevant parties and promotes collaboration among various services and the child's family.

Blended Families with Special Children: Build a Happy Stepfamily

The toolkit presented in this two-book bundle explores the dynamics of stepfamilies caring for children with special needs and disabilities. It presents the information in digestible nuggets ready for consumption by quintessential blended families juggling parenting demands.

You'll discover how to bond with your special stepchild, recognize and embrace the differences, strengthen your family, and maintain a happy relationship with your spouse or partner so that all the children in the family unit feel safe and content.

www.ingramcontent.com/pod-product-compliance
Lightning Source LLC
Chambersburg PA
CBHW050203130526
44591CB00034B/2012